BEYOND
THE CHALLENGE

HOW TO LIVE THE EAGLE SCOUT CHALLENGE

A poem by

RUDYARD KIPLING

Photographs and comments by

DAVID W. WYGANT

HONOR – LOYALTY – COURAGE – CHEERFULNESS - SERVICE

CREDITS

IF—BEYOND THE CHALLENGE
How to Live the Eagle Scout Challenge
By David W. Wygant

Photos: David W. Wygant
Winter Scene Photos: Kathryn E. Stewart
Author of If: Rudyard Kipling 1865-1936
Eagle Challenge, Scout Oath, Scout Laws: Boy Scouts of America

Book Design: David W. Wygant
Jacket Design: David W. Wygant

To order additional copies of this book, contact:
Xlibris
844-714-8691
www.Xlibris.com
Orders@Xlibris.com

ISBN:	Softcover	978-1-4363-2556-1
	Hardcover	978-1-4363-2557-8
	EBook	979-8-3694-1188-9

Library of Congress Control Number: 2008901817

Print information available on the last page

Rev. date: 11/17/2023

HONOR - LOYALTY - COURAGE - CHEERFULNESS - SERVICE

Dedication

I dedicate this book to all Eagle Scouts, and to those who will become Eagles in the future. It is my hope it will guide them to a greater understanding and fulfillment of the Eagle Scout Challenge. I also hope that all Scouts currently on the Eagle Trail will be inspired to continue the journey and become Eagle Scouts themselves.

I dedicate this book to my Grandfather Cecil, my mother and father, Betty and Bill, my brothers, John and Don, their children, Aaron, Daniel, and Melissa, to my children Jacob, Jennifer, Lucas, and Zachary. Jacob and Zachary are Eagle Scouts. Jennifer and Lucas are accomplishing great things too. Both shine with the same eternal Eagle spirit. A father could not be more proud of all his children.

I dedicate this book to Troop 205 Scoutmaster Kay Stewart. Her accomplishments as a "builder of young men" are inspiring as is her dedication to the Scouting program. I dedicate this book to my dear friends John and Joanne Nordale. John is an Eagle himself and his wife Joanne by association and spirit. I dedicate this book to Troop 205 for its commitment to the "patrol method" and the Scouting Spirit as modeled by the Swamp Rhinos (adult patrol), and especially for the many opportunities it has given me to serve.

David W. Wygant

Eagle 1969
Vigil 1972

HONOR – LOYALTY – COURAGE – CHEERFULNESS - SERVICE

BE PREPARED

BSA

HONOR – LOYALTY – COURAGE – CHEERFULNESS - SERVICE

Introduction

The Scouting Movement was started by Robert S.S. Baden Powell in England in 1907 and was soon to become an international inspiration and success. Today, after 100 plus years, there are 28 million Scouts in 216 countries. While these numbers provide a good sense of the Scouting Movement in terms of size and growth, by themselves they don't begin to reflect the positive impact Scouting has had worldwide on the countries, communities, and individuals it has touched.

SCOUTING IN AMERICA

In America the Movement began in 1910. By 2006, Scouting numbered almost 6 million including Scout youth and registered adult volunteers. Well over 110 million American men have benefited from its positive influence on their development and their character. A recent book by Alvin Townley, <u>Legacy of Honor</u>, describes the quiet but pervasive and positive effect Eagle Scouts have had on America. Eagles have lived their lives in our society at all levels often making important contributions wherever they are. Their sense of duty and their values are so well known, that saying someone is an Eagle Scout communicates a very special image which includes the best that America and humanity has to offer.

EAGLES

It is for these Eagles that I have assembled this combination of photographs and the famous words of Rudyard Kipling in his poem "If." Because he wrote "If" in 1895 before the start of the Boy Scout Movement, he couldn't have know at the time that his poem might serve as a "set of instructions" to help Eagle Scouts live their lives according to the Eagle Scout Challenge in which they pledge themselves to Honor, Loyalty, Courage, Cheerfulness and Service. However, because of a number of other close connections Kipling had to Scouting, it makes perfect sense.

RUDYARD KIPLING AND ROBERT S. S. BADEN-POWELL (B-P)

Many people, and certainly most in the Scouting Movement, know that Kipling wrote "The Jungle Book," which is the basis for the Cub Scout program. Beyond that, the extent of Kipling's support of Scouting isn't common knowledge, but it was plentiful. It is also not well known that B-P and Rudyard Kipling were contemporaries in time and had intersecting lives as they became good friends.

Both men were born in the Victorian era, B-P first in 1857, Kipling eight years later. Both men died within five years of each other. B-P died last at age 84 in 1941. Both men attended English public schools and, because of that alone, have much in common. They were both writers and artists, and in the books and stories that they wrote, they created most of their own sketches. The two men first met in Lahore, India, sometime between October 1882 and November 1884. They met through their respective families. Kipling's father and B-P's brother were colleagues in establishing the Museum of Indian Arts and Crafts in Lahore.

It was in 1910 that Kipling published "If", and it was to become one of the most popular poems in the English language. Later, in July of 1916, Baden-Powell wrote to Kipling to ask his permission to use The Jungle Book in his own re-vamp of the Wolf Cub scheme. B-P felt the scheme needed a central story attractive to youngsters, on which to hang specially adapted Scouting teachings. Kipling was in total agreement with B-P's efforts to spread Scouting and through the years did all he could to help. Yet this generosity, as far as his work was concerned, was not characteristic. He was notoriously sensitive about being quoted or exploited. Nonetheless, Kipling sent B-P's drafts back without a single revision. This was true friendship linked by the certainty that, in B-P's hands, his characters would reach a wider audience, gain more popularity and do better for the "Empire" than they ever could if left within the covers of Kipling's own books alone.

HONOR – LOYALTY – COURAGE – CHEERFULNESS – SERVICE

Both men would become world-famous. Winston Churchill wrote about both men in glowing terms, they both received honorary doctorates, and were given the highest honors. Kipling received the Nobel Prize for Literature in 1907. B-P was nominated for the Nobel Prize for Peace in 1939 for his work in 1938, and the preceding thirty years in promoting the "fraternity of the nations through the Boy Scout Movement", but, unfortunately, and for obvious reasons, the Peace Prize was not awarded in 1939.

Upon Kipling's death, B-P wrote, "Our Movement has lost a true and valued friend. From its earliest days Scouting was heartily encouraged by him. He had practically been a life-long friend to me, and I shall miss his cheery, clever and helpful personality."

Kipling was buried along with the other British literary immortals in Westminster Abbey. Baden-Powell was buried, by his own wishes , at Nyeri in Kenya, in spite of the fact that Lady Baden-Powell was offered the opportunity, had she wished, for the "The Founder" to also be buried in Westminster Abbey. It was proposed that his gravestone would be in the main aisle, a unique mark of respect for a commoner. As it ended up, a large commemorative stone was placed in the floor by the internal wall at the main entrance, so in death as in life Baden-Powell and Rudyard Kipling are forever linked.

LIVING THE EAGLE CHALLENGE
In recent years, I have had the privilege of speaking at a number of Eagle Courts of Honor, and on those occasions, I have tried to personalize my remarks to fit the escapades and adventures of the new Eagle. I have also taken these Courts of Honor as opportunities to discuss how Kipling's poem "If" can act as a guide to help the Eagle live out the Eagle Challenge conspicuously in his life. The poem is very direct and predicts many of the challenges the Eagle will face in a life of high standards.

At many Eagle Courts of Honor, attending Eagles are invited to the front to encircle the new Eagle as they pledge themselves to the Eagle Challenge. This is a "welcoming" circle of support that says, "You are one of us now and we're here to support you as those before supported us. We renew our pledges to the Eagle Challenge along with you."

In the Challenge, Eagles pledge themselves to Honor, Loyalty, Courage, Cheerfulness and Service. These words represent lofty ideals not easily lived out in real life. The Eagle Challenge is an "underscore" of other important values and principles found in the Scout Oath and the Scout Law. Living with them as a guide is not easy. Kipling's poem "If" helps bring it all down to earth. It is very direct and simple. It is practical and makes sense. While difficult, it is doable. Having started with The Jungle Book, which became the basis of Cub Scouts, it is fitting that another of Kipling's writings should have the last guiding word at the pinnacle of Scouting.

CONCLUSION
This book was written for Eagle Scouts. Nonetheless, it is my hope that anyone who finds meaning in the Eagle Scout Challenge on the next page will also find meaning in this presentation of "If." The individuals who find such meaning will help make a better world for all of us, as they live happier and more fulfilling lives.

In life's journey, success is important and can be rightly measured a number of different ways. By their nature, Eagles tend to find success. However, having impact and making a difference is better than success, and longer lasting. Work to lead a life that makes a difference.

Always remember, the calling of an Eagle is to fly high, see far and serve.

HONOR – LOYALTY – COURAGE – CHEERFULNESS - SERVICE

Eagle Scout Challenge

The foremost responsibility of an Eagle Scout is to live with **honor**. To an Eagle Scout, **honor** is the foundation of all character. He knows that "A Scout is trustworthy" is the very first point of the Scout Law for a good reason. An Eagle Scout lives honorably, not only because **honor** is important to him but because of the vital significance of the example he sets for other Scouts. Living honorably reflects credit on his home, his church, his troop, and his community. May the white of the Eagle badge remind you to always live with **honor**.

The second obligation of an Eagle Scout is **loyalty**. A Scout is true to his family, Scout leaders, friends, school, and nation. His **loyalty** to his troop and brother Scouts makes him pitch in and carry his share of the load. All of these help to build the **loyalty** which means devotion to community, to country, to one's own ideals, and to God. Let the blue of the Eagle badge always inspire your **loyalty**.

The third obligation of an Eagle Scout is to be **courageous**. Courage has always been a quality by which men measure themselves and others. To a Scout, bravery means not only the courage to face physical danger, but the determination to stand up for the right. Trusting in God, with faith in his fellowman, he looks forward to each day, seeking his share of the world's work to do. Let the red of the Eagle badge remind you always of courage.

The fourth obligation of an Eagle Scout is to be **cheerful**. To remind the Eagle Scout to always wear a smile, the red, white, and blue ribbon is attached to the scroll of the Second Class Scout award, which has its ends turned up in a smile.

The final responsibility of an Eagle Scout is service. The Eagle Scout extends a helping hand to those who still toil up Scouting's trail, just as others helped him in his climb to the Eagle. The performance of the daily Good Turn takes on a new meaning when he enters a more adult life of continuing service to others.

The Eagle stands as protector of the weak and helpless. He aids and comforts the unfortunate and the oppressed. He upholds the rights of others while defending his own. He will always "Be Prepared" to put forth his best.

You deserve much credit for having achieved Scouting's highest award. But wear your award with humility, ever mindful that the Eagle Scout is looked up to as an example. May the Scout Oath and the Scout Law be your guide for tomorrow and onward.

HONOR - LOYALTY - COURAGE - CHEERFULNESS - SERVICE

You can keep your head when all about you
Are losing theirs and blaming it on you,

HONOR – LOYALTY – COURAGE – CHEERFULNESS – SERVICE

If

You can trust yourself when all men doubt you
But make allowance for their doubting too,

If

You can wait and not be tired by waiting,
Or being lied about, don't deal in lies,
Or being hated, don't give way to hating,
And yet don't look too good, nor talk too wise:

HONOR - LOYALTY - COURAGE - CHEERFULNESS - SERVICE

If

You can dream—and not make dreams your master,

If

You can think—and not make thoughts your aim;

HONOR – LOYALTY – COURAGE – CHEERFULNESS – SERVICE

You can meet with Triumph and Disaster
And treat those two impostors just the same;

You can bear to hear the truth you've spoken
Twisted by knaves to make a trap for fools,

HONOR – LOYALTY – COURAGE – CHEERFULNESS – SERVICE

Many Point Grace

For our camp, its lake and trees.
For our food and daily needs.
For the wonders of Many Point
We give you thanks, oh Lord.

Presented by the ⬛⬛⬛ Committees

Or

Watch the things you gave your life to, broken,
And stoop and build 'em up with worn-out tools:

HONOR – LOYALTY – COURAGE – CHEERFULNESS – SERVICE

If

You can make one heap of all your winnings
And risk it all on one turn of pitch-and-toss,

And

Lose, and start again at your beginnings
And never breath a word about your loss;

If

You can force your heart and nerve and sinew
To serve your turn long after they are gone,

HONOR – LOYALTY – COURAGE – CHEERFULNESS - SERVICE

And

So hold on when there is nothing in you
Except the Will which says to them: "Hold on!"

If

You can talk with crowds and keep your virtue,
Or walk with kings—nor lose the common touch,

JACKSON ABIDE

If

Neither foes nor loving friends can hurt you;

If

All men count with you, but none too much,

If

You can fill the unforgiving minute
With sixty seconds' worth of distance run,

Yours

Is the Earth and everything that's in it,
And—which is more—you'll be a Man, my son!

HONOR – LOYALTY – COURAGE – CHEERFULNESS - SERVICE

HONOR – LOYALTY – COURAGE – CHEERFULNESS - SERVICE

"B.P.'S" LAST MESSAGE

Dear Scouts,

If you have ever seen the play Peter Pan you will remember how the pirate chief was always making his dying speech because he was afraid that possibly when the time came for him to die he might not have time to get it off his chest. It is much the same with me, and so, although I am not at this moment dying, I shall be doing so one of these days and I want to send you a parting word of good-bye.

Remember, it is the last you will ever hear from me, so think it over.

I have had a most happy life and I want each one of you to have as happy a life too.

I believe that God put us in this jolly world to be happy and enjoy life. Happiness doesn't come from being rich, nor merely from being successful in your career, nor by self-indulgence. One step towards happiness is to make yourself healthy and strong while you are a boy, so that you can be useful and so can enjoy life when you are a man.

Nature study will show you how full of beautiful and wonderful things God has made the world for you to enjoy. Be contented with what you have got and make the best of it. Look on the bright side of things instead of the gloomy one.

But the real way to get happiness is by giving out happiness to other people. Try and leave this world a little better than you found it and when your turn comes to die, you can die happy in feeling that at any rate you have not wasted your time but have done your best.

"Be Prepared" in this way, to live happy and to die happy—stick to your Scout promise always—even after you have ceased to be a boy—and God help you to do it.

Your friend,

Baden-Powell

SCOUT OATH

On my honor I will do my best
To do my duty to God and my country

and to obey the Scout Law;

To help other people at all times;

To keep myself physically strong,

mentally awake, and morally straight.

SCOUT LAW

TRUSTWORTHY A Scout tells the truth. He keeps his promises. Honesty is part of his code of conduct. People can depend on him.

LOYAL A Scout is true to his family, Scout leaders, friends, school, and nation.

HELPFUL A Scout is concerned about other people. He does things willingly for others without pay or reward.

FRIENDLY A Scout is a friend to all. He is a brother to other Scouts. He seeks to understand others. He respects those with ideas and customs other than his own.

COURTEOUS A Scout is polite to everyone regardless of age or position. He knows good manners make it easier for people to get along together.

KIND A Scout understands there is strength in being gentle. He treats others as he wants to be treated. He does not hurt or kill harmless things without reason.

OBEDIENT A Scout follows the rules of his family, school, and troop. He obeys the laws of his community and country. If he thinks these rules and laws are unfair, he tries to have them changed in an orderly manner rather than disobey them.

CHEERFUL A Scout looks for the bright side of things. He cheerfully does tasks that come his way. He tries to make others happy.

THRIFTY A Scout works to pay his way and to help others. He saves for unforeseen needs. He protects and conserves natural resources. He carefully uses time and property.

BRAVE A Scout can face danger even if he is afraid. He has the courage to stand for what he thinks is right even if others laugh at or threaten him.

CLEAN A Scout keeps his body and mind fit and clean. He goes around with those who believe in living by these same ideals. He helps keep his home and community clean.

REVERENT A Scout is reverent toward God. He is faithful in his religious duties. He respects the beliefs of others.

HONOR – LOYALTY – COURAGE – CHEERFULNESS – SERVICE

BE PREPARED

B S A

Printed in the United States
by Baker & Taylor Publisher Services